What Color Is It?
Quo colore est?

"I Am Reading Latin" Series

This is one of a series of Latin books developed for ages 4–8. Other books include

What Will I Eat?
How Many Animals?
Who Loves Me?

Check www.bolchazy.com for more information.
Recordings of these books also will be on the website.

Why learn Latin?

A short answer is that Latin
- develops a person's English
- provides a solid foundation for the acquisition of other languages
- connects us with the cultures of 57 nations on 4 continents
- provides us with cultural roots and a sense of identity
- enhances our career choices

Latin vocabulary forms the basis of 60% of the words in the English language, and it also forms the roots of the Spanish, French, and Italian languages. The very act of learning Latin serves to increase the mind's analytic processes, and an exposure to the Roman world constitutes a journey back to the roots of our own Western heritage. It's never too early to start learning Latin.

An I Am Reading Latin Book

What Color Is It?
Quo colore est?

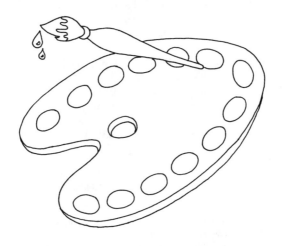

by Marie Carducci Bolchazy

translated by Mardah B. C. Weinfield
illustrated by Yana Igorevna Myaskovskaya
designed by Adam Phillip Velez

Bolchazy-Carducci Publishers, Inc.
Wauconda, Illinois USA

This publication was made possible by
PEGASUS LIMITED.

© Copyright 2003, by Bolchazy-Carducci Publishers, Inc.
All rights reserved.

Printed in the United States of America
2003
by United Graphics

BOLCHAZY-CARDUCCI PUBLISHERS, INC.
1000 Brown Street, Unit 101
Wauconda, Illinois 60084 U.S.A.
www.bolchazy.com

ISBN: 0-86516-539-4

Library of Congress Cataloging-in-Publication Data

Bolchazy, Marie Carducci.
    What color is it? = Quo colore est : Latin/English version / by Marie Carducci Bolchazy
        p. cm. — (An I am reading Latin book)
    Summary: Introduces the Latin words for a wide range of colors, as well as such related
words as apple, flower, pet, and food.
    ISBN 0-86516-539-4
    1. Latin language—Readers—Juvenile literature. 2. Colors, Words for—Juvenile literature.
[1. Latin languate—Readers. 2. Color.] I. Title: Quo colore est?. II Title.

PA2095.B57 2003
478.6'421—dc21

                                                                          2003045177

Colores, colores, ubique!

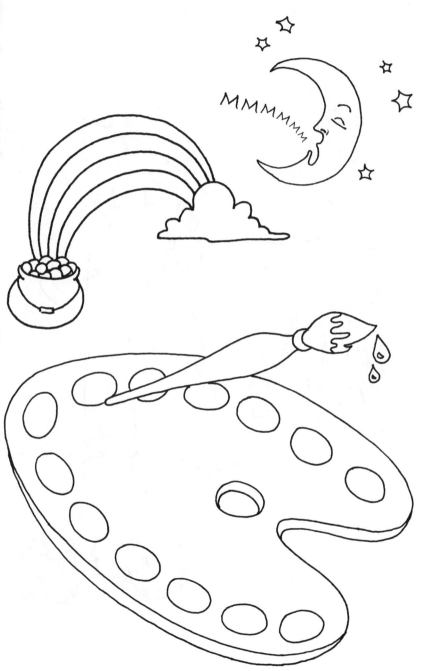

Quo colore est?

Malum rubrum
esse potest

aut citreum quoque

aut etiam viride.

Mala multis coloribus sunt.

Mihi mala rubra sunt optima.

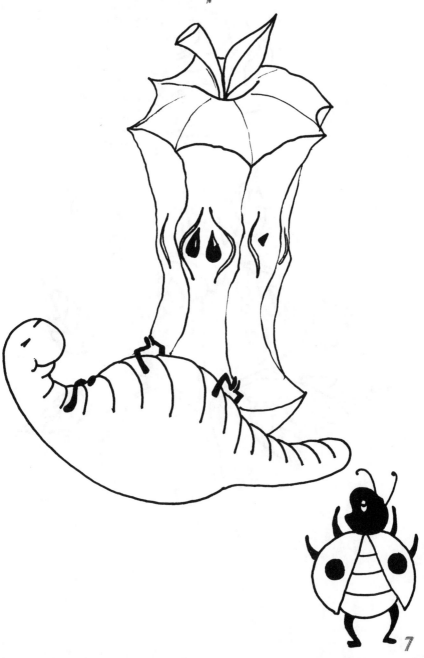

Flos ruber esse potest

vel citreus

vel azureus

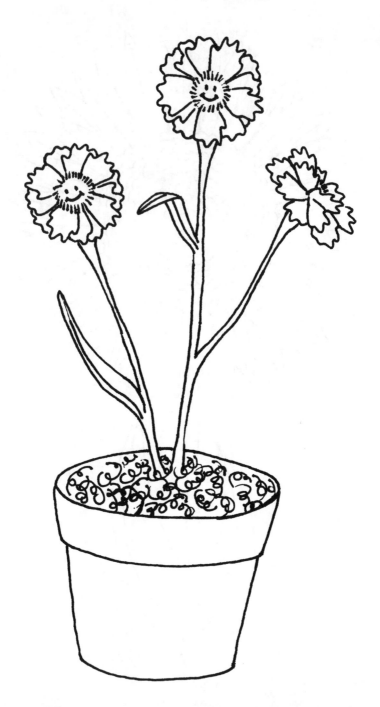

vel salmoneus

vel lacteus.

Flores paene omnibus coloribus esse possunt.

Mihi flos salmoneus est optimus.

Ego delicia paene ubique video.

Delicium atrum esse potest

vel aurantiacum

vel lacteum

vel atrum lacteumque

vel fuscum

vel fumeum

sed non purpureum!

Delicium meum est...

lacteum. atrum. fuscum.

aurantiacum. fumeam.

Imago Meorum Deliciorum

Cibus, cibus, cibus mirabilis!

Cibus fuscus esse potest

ac lacteus

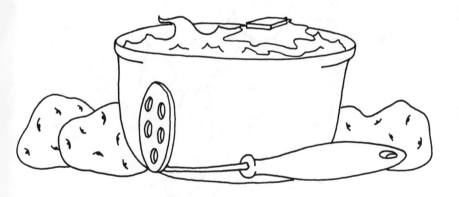

atque viridis

ac ruber

ac purpureus.

Cave cibum atrum!

EDAMUS!

Ego aves omnibus coloribus diligo.

Avis fusca esse potest

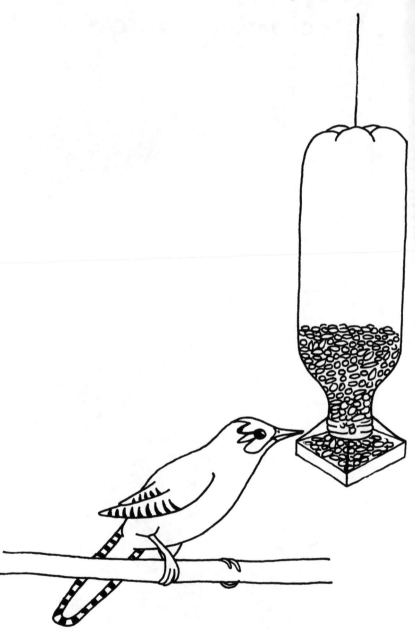

vel atra lacteaque

vel azurea

vel citrea

vel viridis...

Avis multis coloribus esse potest.

Fringilla mea est citrea.

Mihi aves citreae sunt optimae.

Mihi color praeoptatus est

○ ruber

  ○ aurantiacus

○ citreus

  ○ viridis

○ azureus

  ○ purpureus

○ salmoneus

  ○ lacteus

○ fumeus

  ○ fuscus

○ ater

Pinge imaginem colore tibi praeoptato utens.

ruber, rubra, rubrum

aurantiacus, aurantiaca, aurantiacum

citreus, citrea,
citreum

viridis, viridis, viride

azureus, azurea, azureum

purpureus, purpurea, purpureum

salmoneus, salmonea, salmoneum

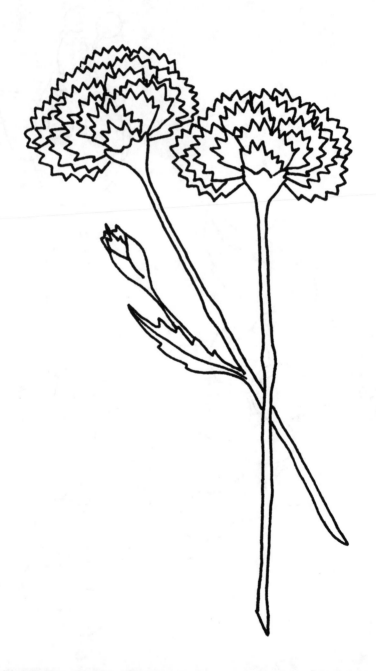

lacteus, lactea, lacteum

fumeus, fumea, fumeum

fuscus, fusca, fuscum

ater, atra, atrum

Translation

TRANSLATOR'S NOTE: As you read this book, you will notice different endings on the names of the colors. This is because, in Latin, colors are adjectives, and adjectives change their endings depending upon the gender of the noun described. Examples are: red flower = *flos ruber;* red bird = *avis rubra;* red apple = *malum rubrum.*

In addition, only the most general Latin word has been used to describe each English color in this book. For example, the color *viridis* has been used to describe an apple, an olive, and a parrot, even though the shade, tint, and hue of the color may vary. A Roman, by contrast, would have used individual color names for each item above: *saligneus* for apple-green, *olivaceus* for olive-green and *psittaceus* for parrot-green. However, as an introduction to colors in Latin, it was decided to emphasize one name for each color, a name that had a recognizable English derivative.

Page	Latin	English
Title	Quo colore est?	What Color Is It?
1	Colores, colores, ubique! MMMMMM	Colors, colors, everywhere! ZZZZZZ
2	Quo colore est?	What color is it?
3	Malum rubrum esse potest	An apple can be red
4	aut citreum quoque	but also yellow
5	aut etiam viride.	and also green.
6	Mala multis coloribus sunt.	Apples are many colors.
7	Mihi mala rubra sunt optima.	To me, red apples are the best.
8	Flos ruber esse potest	A flower can be red
9	vel citreus	or yellow
10	vel azureus	or blue
11	vel salmoneus	or pink
12	vel lacteus.	or white.
13	Flores paene omnibus coloribus esse possunt.	Flowers can be almost any color.
14	Mihi flos salmoneus est optimus.	To me, a pink flower is best.
15	Ego delicia paene ubique video.	I see pets almost everywhere.
16	Delicium atrum esse potest Latrax	A pet can be black Barky (on tag)
17	vel aurantiacum	or orange
18	vel lacteum	or white
19	vel atrum lacteumque	or black and white
20	vel fuscum	or brown
21	vel fumeum Felix	or gray Meowy (on tag)
22	sed non purpureum!	but not purple!
23	Delicium meum est... lacteum. atrum. fuscum. aurantiacum. fumeam.	My pet is... white. black. brown. orange. gray.

24	Imago Meorum Deliciorum Esca Piscaria	A Picture of My Pets Fish Food (on label)
25	Cibus, cibus, cibus mirabilis! Edamus!	Food, food, wonderful food! Let's eat! (on shirt)
26	Cibus fuscus esse potest	Food can be dark brown
27	ac lacteus	and white
28	atque viridis	and green
29	ac ruber	and red
30	ac purpureus.	and purple.
31	Cave cibum atrum!	Beware of black food!
32	EDAMUS!	LET'S EAT!
33	Ego aves omnibus coloribus diligo.	I love birds of all colors.
34	Avis fusca esse potest	A bird can be brown
35	vel atra lacteaque	or black and white
36	vel azurea	or blue
37	vel citrea	or yellow
38	vel viridis...	or green...
39	Avis multis coloribus esse potest.	A bird can be many colors.
40	Fringilla mea est citrea.	My canary is yellow.
41	Mihi aves citreae sunt optimae.	To me, yellow birds are the best.
42	Mihi color praeoptatus est ruber aurantiacus citreus viridis azureus purpureus salmoneus lacteus fumeus fuscus ater	My favorite color is red orange yellow green blue purple pink white gray brown black
43	Pinge imaginem colore tibi praeoptato utens.	Draw a picture using your favorite color.
44	ruber, rubra, rubrum	Red
45	aurantiacus, aurantiaca, aurantiacum	Orange
46	citreus, citrea, citreum	Yellow
47	viridis, viridis, viride	Green
48	azureus, azurea, azureum	Blue
49	purpureus, purpurea, purpureum	Purple
50	salmoneus, salmonea, salmoneum	Pink
51	lacteus, lactea, lacteum	White
52	fumeus, fumea, fumeum	Gray
53	fuscus, fusca, fuscum	Brown
54	ater, atra, atrum	Black

Pronunciation Guide

Symbol	Key Words
ā	April, later, wait
ä	father, not
e	elephant, met, merry
ē	either, feet, honey
i	sit, mitten
ī	icy, kind, my
ō	over, most, load
ô	awful, paw, forget
o͞o	goose, ooze
u	umbrella, sun, mother
ʉ	serpent, surface
ə	a in comma
	e in supper
	i in Marilyn
	o in control
	u in circus

Note about the Latin Forms for Color Words

You will see that we have used three forms for each color. For example, we have listed *ruber, rubra,* and *rubrum* for the word "red." Most of the color words in this book have one or more of the forms we show you on pages 44-54, but there are many other forms we are not showing you. In Latin, each color is an adjective and must match the noun it is describing. With this book, you will have a good start on color words.

Glossary

Derivative English words listed in CAPITALS.

ac (äk) and

ater, atra, atrum (ä′ tär) black ATRABILIOUS, ATRAMENTOUS

atque (ät′ kwə) and

aurantiacus, -a, -um (ô rän tē ä′ kəs) orange

aut (ôt) but, and

avis, -is (ä′ wis) bird AVIAN, AVIARY, AVIATION, AVIATOR, AVICULTURE

azureus, -a, -um (ä zʉ′ re əs) blue AZURE, AZURITE

caveo, -ere, cavi, cautum (kä′ we ō) beware of CAUTION, CAUTIOUS, CAVEAT

cibus, -i (ki′ bəs) food KIBBLE, CIBARIAL

citreus, -a, -um (ki tre′ əs) yellow CITRUS, CITRIC, CITRON, CITROELLA, CITRINE

color, -is (kô′ lôr) color COLOR, COLORANT, COLORATURA, COLORING

delicium, -i (dā li′ ki əm) pet DELICATE, DELICACY

delineo, -are, -avi, -atum (de li′ ne ō) draw DELINEATE

diligo, -ligere, -lexi, -lectum (di′ li gō) love DELIGHT, DELIGHTFUL

edamus   edo, edere, (esse), edi, esum (e dä′ məs) eat EDIBLE

ego (e′ gō) I EGO, EGOISM, EGOTISTICAL

esca piscaria, escae piscariae (es′ kä pis cä′ ri ə) fish food PISCES, PISCATORIAL, PISCINE

esse   sum, esse, fui, futurum (es′ sə) to be ESSENCE, FUTURE

est   sum, esse, fui, futurum (est) is

etiam (et′ i əm) also

Felix   felio, -ire, -ivi, -itum (fā′ lēks) meow "Meowy" FELINE, FELICITY

flos, floris (flōs) flower FLORAL, FLORA, FLORESCENCE, FLORET, FLORID, FLORIST

fringilla, -ae (frin gi′ lə) canary FRINGILLID

fumeus, -a, -um (foo′ me əs) gray FUME, FUMAROLE, FUMIGATE, FUMITORY

fuscus, -a, -um (foos kəs) brown FUSCOUS, OBFUSCATE

imago, -inis (i mä′ gō) likeness, portrait IMAGE, IMAGERY, IMAGINE, IMAGINARY, IMAGINATION

lacteus, -a, -um (läk′ tā əs) white LACTIC, LACTOSE, LACTATE

Latrax   latro, -are, -avi, -atum (lä′ träks) bark "Barky"

malum, -i (mä′ ləm) apple MALIC ACID, MALATE

meus, -a, -um (me′ əs) my

mihi (mē′ hē) to me

mirabilis, -is, -e (mi rä′ bi ləs) wonderful ADMIRABLE

multus, -a, -um (mul′ təs) much, many MULTI-, MULTIPLE, MULTIPLY, MULTITUDE

non (nōn) not

omnis, -is, -e (ôm′ nəs) every, all OMNI-, OMNIPOTENT, OMNISCIENT, OMNIVORE

optimus, -a, -um (ôp′ ti məs) best OPTIMUM, OPTIMAL, OPTIMISTIC, OPTIMIZE

paene (pī′ ne) almost PENUMBRA, PENULTIMATE

pictura, -ae (pik tōō′ rä) picture PICTURE, PICTORAL, PICTURESQUE

pingo, -ngere, -nxi, -ctum (pin′ gō) to paint or draw a picture of DEPICT, PICTURE, PIGMENT

potest   possum, posse, potui (pō′ test) be able POSSIBLE, POSSESS, POTENT, POTENTIAL

praeopto, -are, -avi, -atum (prī ôp′ tō) prefer OPT, OPTION, OPTIONAL

purpureus, -a, -um (pʉr pʉr′ e əs) purple PURPLE, PURPLISH

-que (kwe) and

quo (kwō) what?

quoque (kwō′ kwə) also

ruber, rubra, rubrum (rōō′ bär) red RUBRIC, RUBY, RUBELLA, RUBESCENT, ROUGE

salmoneus, -a, -um (säl mô′ ne əs) pink SALMON, SALMONOID

sed (sed) but

sunt   sum, esse, fui, futurum (sunt) are

tibi (ti′ bē) to you, for you

tuus, -a, -um (tōō′ əs) your

ubique (ōō bē′ kwə) everywhere UBIQUITOUS, UBIQUITY

ullus, -a, -um (u′ ləs) any

utens   utor, uti, usus sum (ōō′ tənz) using USE, USEABLE, UTILITY, UTILE, UTILIZE, UTILITARIAN, UTENSIL

vel (wel) or

video, -ere, vidi, visum (wi′ de ō) see VIDEO, VISION, VISIONARY, VISIBLE, VISUAL, VISIBILITY

viridis, -is, -e (wi′ ri dəs) green VIRID, VIRIDESCENT, VIRIDIAN, VIRIDITY

Acknowledgements

We thank the officials of Wheeling High School in District 214 in Wheeling, Illinois for supporting the art in this book.

The illustrations in this book were arranged for by artist and teacher Thom Kapheim. We also thank Mary Pride, author of *Practical Home School Magazine*, for her suggestion that we develop Latin books for young children. Both Terence Tunberg and John Traupman reviewed the Latin for accuracy.

About the Author

Marie Carducci Bolchazy has a doctoral degree in education from the State University of New York at Albany and a masters degree, also in education, from Cornell University. She currently works full-time at Bolchazy-Carducci Publishers, owned by her husband and her. One of their specialties is Latin books. Customers frequently asked for Latin books for primary-level Latin, and the "I Am Reading Latin" series is her effort to fill that request.

About the Translator

Mardah B.C. Weinfield holds Master of Arts degrees in both Latin and Education. She has been studying and teaching Latin for over twenty years, most recently with her own sons, William and Samuel.

Note about the Illustrator

Yana Igorevna Myaskovskaya was born in Moscow, Russia on April 28th, 1987. She immigrated to the Northwest suburbs of Chicago when she was four years old and continues to speak Russian fluently. Yana is currently a sophomore at Wheeling High School, where her favorite subjects include biology, history, and of course, art.